MR. PISSHEAD

Published by Lekker Publishing

Mr Pisshead liked to drink.

In fact Mr Pisshead loved to drink, and the more he drank the more rude he became.

The trouble was, the more rude he became, the more he drank.

And so it went on.

Mr Pisshead lived in a house that looked rather like himself.

It was a messy, trashed looking sort of house.

One afternoon, Mr Pisshead awoke rather later than usual.

His head had been pumping all night long, as usual, and that had made him wake up feeling dehydrated, as usual.

So Mr Pisshead got up, went downstairs, and made himself a drink...or two.

12
9
3
6

This is what Mr Pisshead had:

Vodka- 4 shots
Lager- 6 bottles
Whiskey- 2 shots
Wine- 3 glasses
Cider- 2 pints

When he had finished Mr Pisshead fell back in his chair, smiled a very pissed sort of smile and thought.

"Now I wonder what would be nice to have next?"

But before he could answer, he fell into a deep sleep, snoring and dribbling as usual.

He didn't even hear the postman posting two party invitations through the letterbox.

Lucky Mr Pisshead.

He was invited to two parties that very same evening, one thrown by the naughtiest Misters in town and the other by the most boring Misters in town.

Now which party would he go to?

Mr Pisshead knew instantly which one he would prefer to attend. But.... his vision was so blurred he got the addresses all mixed up.

Mr Spike
No.10
Rave Side
Mr Straight
No.2
Neat Street

Poor Mr Pisshead.

When he arrived at the party and saw Mr Straight, Mr Boring, Mr Dull and Mr Know-It-All he couldn't believe his eyes and groaned inwardly at his terrible mistake.

He couldn't see a drop of booze in sight and so he turned around and left, giving them the V's. Just like that!

Luckily, the other party was just over the road. Mr Pisshead could hear the music blaring from the windows.

He crossed the road and knocked on the door.

'Ciao!' said Mr Spike who was holding a Pina Colada in his hand.

Mr Pisshead went inside and was very happy to see Mr Rave, who was spinning some excellent tunes, Mr Extreme, Mr M. Mushroom and Mr Digital.

"No ladies?" asked Mr Pisshead, heading straight to the bar.

Just as Mr Pisshead was necking his first pint there was a knock at the door.

In came Little Miss Chuckle, Little Miss Hellraiser and Little Miss Loudmouth.

'Now we're talking', said Mr Pisshead rubbing his hands together and licking his lips.

Then in walked his sister, Little Miss Pisshead.

"What the f...?" groaned Mr Pisshead, disappointed that his sibling had arrived to report any misbehaviour to his mother, Mrs Pisshead.

In order to cope with the mixed feelings of excitement and disappointment, Mr Pisshead drank four glasses of champagne, three shots of tequila, two pints of real ale and a Margarita.

Oh dear we all know what happens to Mr Pisshead when he starts drinking don't we?

First of all, he bumped into everyone, spilling their drinks, then he dropped his own drink smashing glass everywhere, then he started doing the conga, on his own, then he told some very tasteless jokes and THEN he did a wee behind the curtain. And THAT was just the beginning!

Mr Pisshead was not only off his head, he was completely twatted, rat-arsed, shit-faced....

Knock, knock, knock. The next door neighbour appeared at the door.

It was Mr Crank. ‘Turn the music down’ he said, ‘or I’ll call the police’.

Mr Pisshead slowly but decisively raised his middle finger.

Mr Crank gasped in shock at this offensive gesture and immediately dialled the number of his bouncer friend, Mr Knuckle.

Along came Mr Knuckle and gave Mr Pisshead a knuckle sandwich that sent him flying through the air.

Little Miss Chuckle, Little Miss Hellraiser, Little Miss Loudmouth AND his horrified sibling, Little Miss Pisshead, all agreed that Mr Pisshead needed to be taught a lesson.

They called someone they knew might be able to help.

The Fat Wizard! Why hadn't they thought of him before? He'd always been able to solve the other Mister's problems.

The Fat Wizard appeared in an instant. Mr Pisshead rubbed his eyes in disbelief.

“From now on”, said the Fat Wizard, “the minute you drink alcohol, your pants will fall down”.

And he cast his spell just like that.

The next day, Mr Pisshead woke up to the sound of someone knocking on the door of his messy, rather trashed looking sort of house. He went downstairs, and made himself a quick drink or two (a pair of vodka shots), then went to open the door, all in his own time.

'Good Morning' said Mrs Pisshead, his mother.
"Your sister told me you were poorly so I thought I would drop by to see if you were feeling any better?"

Oh dear, the Fat Wizard's spell suddenly took terrible effect.

Oops.